Who Was
Nikola Tesla?

by Jim Gigliotti

illustrated by John Hinderliter

Penguin Workshop

For Sophia, our creative genius—JG

For Eli and Anna. Your dad thinks you're the greatest kids a dad could ask for—JH

PENGUIN WORKSHOP
An Imprint of Penguin Random House LLC, New York

Text copyright © 2018 by Jim Gigliotti.
Illustrations copyright © 2018 by Penguin Random House LLC. All rights reserved.
Published by Penguin Workshop, an imprint of Penguin Random House LLC, New York.
PENGUIN and PENGUIN WORKSHOP are trademarks of Penguin Books Ltd.
WHO HQ & Design is a registered trademark of Penguin Random House LLC.
Manufactured in China.

Visit us online at www.penguinrandomhouse.com.

Library of Congress Control Number: 2018038825

ISBN 9780448488592   10 9 8 7 6 5 4 3 2

Part of the *What Is Science & Technology?* Boxed Set, ISBN 9780593090138

Contents

Who Was Nikola Tesla?

Nikola Tesla was seven years old on the day the people of Gospić, in what is now modern-day Croatia, received a brand-new fire pump. The town had organized a fire department for the very first time. The firefighters trained hard to learn to work together. But it was the fire pump that everyone wanted to see. It was a really big deal. The pump let firefighters move water from the local river and direct it onto flames, in order to put out fires quickly.

The leaders of the town organized a celebration
to show off the fire pump. Everyone in Gospić
(say: GAH-spich) put on their best Sunday
clothes. They gathered around when the machine
was brought down to the river. There was a
ceremony, and several people gave speeches. Then

came the big moment: a demonstration to show how the pump could spray water.

The new machine was painted black and red. It needed sixteen men to work it. They took their positions, turned on the hose, and . . . nothing! No water came out. The pump didn't work!

None of the grown-ups was sure what to do. But young Nikola (say: NEEK-oh-la) had an idea. "I know what to do, mister," he told one of the men in charge. "You keep pumping." Nikola jumped into the water and felt for the hose. There was no pressure. He tried to picture the reason in his mind. He thought something might be blocking it.

Quickly, Nikola found the problem. The hose had bent sharply in one spot and stopped the pressure from pushing the water out. He straightened out the line, and water surged through the hose! The crowd cheered. Many of the people got wet! But they didn't mind. Nikola was a hero. They carried him on their shoulders.

Before Nikola jumped into the river that day in the early 1860s, he didn't know anything about fire pumps or water pressure. He just knew there was some reason the machine was not working properly—and he knew he could figure out a way to fix it.

Nikola never lost his gift for figuring things out. He grew up to be one of the most important inventors in the history of the world! He helped create the technology that led to radios and remote-control devices. He imagined cell phones and the Internet many years before anyone heard of such things. He created a motor that helped power machines around the world. And he is most famous for helping to bring electricity into homes everywhere.

Nikola had a talent for picturing a problem in his mind and figuring out a way to fix it. Luckily for us, he loved to develop new and better ways of making things work.

CHAPTER 1
Learning Experiences

Young Nikola Tesla was a very smart boy who one day did something not very smart: He tried to fly. He went out to the barn at his family's farm carrying an umbrella. He climbed to the roof of the barn, opened the umbrella, and jumped off.

Not surprisingly, Nikola fell directly to the ground with a thud. Fortunately, he didn't break any bones. He spent several weeks recovering from the fall. Then he was as good as new.

Nikola wasn't even six years old at the time. There was no such thing as an airplane then. He didn't know about gravity or lift or the forces that allow things to fly. He didn't know it was *not* possible to fly simply by holding an umbrella in the air! The only thing Nikola knew was that he could picture himself floating through the air with his umbrella. And if he could picture something in his mind, he believed he could make it work.

The Tesla family farm where Nikola tried to fly that day was in a village known as Smiljan. That's where Nikola had been born in 1856. Smiljan is in what is now known as the country of Croatia. But Nikola's family was Serbian. Serbia is a neighboring country.

Nikola's father was Milutin (say: mil-YOU-tin),

the priest in the local Serbian Orthodox Church. Orthodox priests can be married and have children. Milutin wanted Nikola to be a priest just like he was. Nikola's mother was named Djouka (say: DYOH-kah). She ran the family farm and had never gone to school.

Djouka had never even learned to read or write. Her mother had become blind when Djouka was still a young girl and—as the eldest daughter in the family—she took over running the household. There had been no time for school.

But Djouka was a very intelligent woman who had an incredible memory. Word for word, she could remember stories from the Bible and poems she had heard. Her husband was an educated man who wrote poetry, owned many books, and spoke German and Italian in addition to his native Serbian-Croatian language. Milutin probably recited many of his books to her.

Djouka worked tirelessly from dawn until dark around the farm. She often used tools that she invented herself, such as a mechanical eggbeater. "I must trace to my mother's influence whatever inventiveness I possess," Nikola once wrote.

Nikola had two older sisters, Milka and Angelina, and one younger sister, Marica. He also had a brother, Dane, who was seven years older. Tragically, he was killed in an accident involving the family horse when he was only twelve years old. Like Nikola, Dane had been very smart.

Nikola's birthday was July 10. Most accounts say he was born just as the clock struck midnight, turning July 9 into July 10. Outside, a thunderstorm flashed lightning in the sky.

The flare of lightning at his birth was appropriate, because electricity soon fascinated Nikola. When he was three years old, he loved to play with Macak, the family cat. One cold, dry day while he stroked Macak's fur, he saw little sparks. Nikola was amazed! He didn't understand what the sparks were at the time, but he knew he wanted to find out. "It's electricity," his father explained. "The same thing you see through trees in a storm."

Nikola followed his mother's example by experimenting and coming up with his own ideas. When he was four, he developed his first "invention." One day, the other boys in the village went fishing, but they didn't take Nikola with them. Determined not to miss out on all the fun, Nikola made his own fishing line with a hook on the end of a string. He didn't have bait to tempt the fish. His homemade line didn't work. But while Nikola was trying to figure out what went wrong, a frog leaped at the hook. Nikola grabbed him. It turned out that his fishing line was really a frog-catcher! He returned to the farm with nearly two dozen frogs that day. All the boys in the neighborhood liked to play with frogs.

His friends hadn't caught a single fish! But they were happy to learn Nikola's secret for catching frogs.

When he was five, Nikola began going to school in the village. He studied math, religion, and German. Outside the classroom, he was always learning, too. Once, when Nikola was playing down by a stream in the village, he noticed a small slice of a tree trunk shaped like a circle. Nikola cut a hole through the center of the wood. He found a tree branch and pushed that through the hole. Then he rested the ends of the branch on the opposite banks of the stream. The slice of the tree trunk was partly in the water. The wheel began to spin!

The force of the water made the wheel turn round and round. Nikola had taken energy from nature (the stream) and generated enough power to spin the wheel around!

CHAPTER 2
Scientific Mind

The Tesla farm had many types of animals, including chickens, sheep, and geese. Nikola especially liked to watch the geese. In perfect formation, they flew off each morning to their feeding grounds. In perfect formation, they came back at sundown.

It was a shock to seven-year-old Nikola when the family moved to the nearby town of Gospić. His father had been sent there by his church to become the pastor of the town's Orthodox parish. A pastor is the religious leader of a certain region or community. Gospić was only a few miles away from Smiljan. But for Nikola, it was a world of difference.

Gospić was much bigger than his cozy village had been. And many more people lived there.

The Tesla family lived in a house in Gospić, not on a farm. Nikola had loved going into the woods of Smiljan. He liked to play by the stream, experimenting with his waterwheels. But in this new town, Nikola was too shy to wander from the house much at all. "I would rather have faced a roaring lion than one of the city dudes who strolled about," he said.

But Nikola was required to go to his father's church every Sunday. He was glad to be given the job of ringing the bells before and after each service. It meant going up into the bell tower, called a belfry, away from the "city dudes."

Before the church service began, Nikola would race up the steps to the belfry to ring the bell. After the service was over and everyone had left the church, he raced back down the steps.

One day, Nikola didn't realize that not quite everyone had left the church. A wealthy woman in a fancy dress was making her way outside. She had stopped to talk with Milutin. Nikola barreled down the steps, three at a time. He took his last leap and, to his dismay, saw that he was heading straight for the long edge of the woman's dress that trailed behind her as she walked. It was a direct hit. The back of the dress tore off with such a great ripping sound that many of the churchgoers rushed back inside to see what had happened. The woman was furious. Milutin was embarrassed. And Nikola was in trouble.

After that, Nikola felt as if no one in town wanted to even talk to him! He worried about

it for a long time. He didn't feel forgiven until he became the hero of the day for being smart enough to fix the hose on the new fire pump.

In Gospić, Nikola completed his elementary schooling during the day. At night, he read the books in his father's library. "Of all things, I liked books the best," he said. Nikola would stay up late into the night reading. His father thought Nikola was going to ruin his eyesight. Milutin thought that maybe Nikola liked books a little too much! He took away the candles Nikola needed to read at night.

So Nikola went to his room and made his own candles. He blocked the space underneath the door and the keyhole so no light could be seen from the outside. Sometimes, he stayed up all night reading, until his mother began her morning chores.

In one book, Nikola read about a place in North America called Niagara Falls. Nikola pictured in his mind a giant waterwheel like the one he had built in his small village stream.

He pictured it at the base of Niagara Falls. If his little homemade waterwheel could work, how much power could a huge wheel powered by the Falls make! Even then, he was imagining technology that didn't yet exist.

Nikola showed his uncle Josip a picture of Niagara Falls. One day, Nikola told his uncle, he would travel to America and make his idea work.

When he was ten years old, Nikola entered the Real Gymnasium in town. In Europe, a gymnasium is another name for a school. Real Gymnasium was Nikola's middle school. The way Nikola did math problems in his head amazed his teachers. They thought he might be cheating. He wasn't, though. When Nikola was given a problem, he easily saw the solution in his mind. To him, visualizing figures in his head was no different than working them out on the board or a piece of paper.

Niagara Falls

Niagara Falls is on the border between Canada and the state of New York in the United States. It was formed when glaciers melted at the end of the last Ice Age, about twelve thousand years ago.

Niagara Falls is actually three waterfalls named the Horseshoe Falls, the American Falls, and the Bridal Veil Falls. The Horseshoe Falls is the highest (167 feet) and the widest (2,600 feet). Together, the three waterfalls drop 3,160 tons of water every second!

CHAPTER 3
His Own Path

In 1866, when Nikola started at Real Gymnasium, it was a "new and fairly well equipped institution," he said. Its classrooms had scientific equipment that was modern for the times. Nikola liked it most when his teachers conducted electrical and mechanical experiments.

He enjoyed his four years there, and he completed the program with high marks. The town leaders in Gospić were impressed. After graduation, they asked him to make a list of all the books they had in the local library.

Before Nikola could get the job done, though, he became very sick. He was forced to stay in bed for weeks at a time. His doctors feared he might die. Nikola spent his time reading books from the library. One day, he discovered a collection of books by Mark Twain. His stories made Nikola laugh. He enjoyed them so much they almost 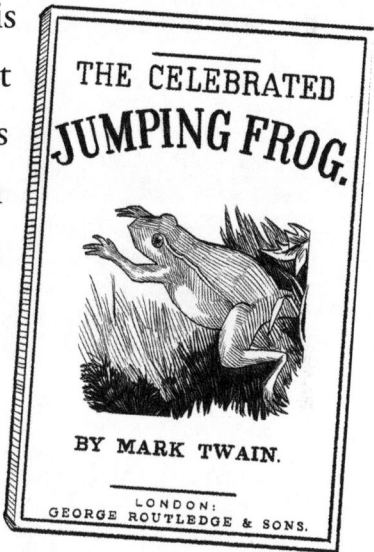 made him forget how sick he was! Mark Twain's books helped Nikola make "the miraculous recovery that followed," he said.

Mark Twain (1835–1910)

Mark Twain is the pen name of Samuel Clemens, an American author and humorist who wrote twenty-eight books and many short stories and essays. At the height of his career, Twain was one of the most famous men in the world.

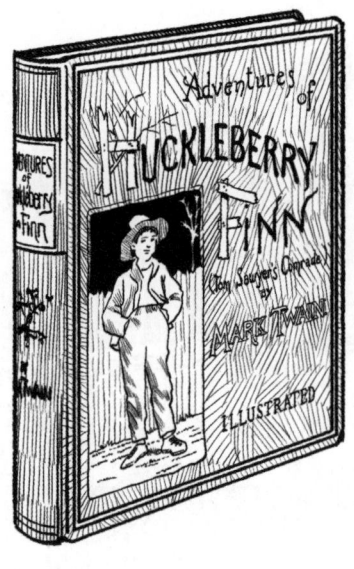

His two best-known novels are *The Adventures of Tom Sawyer* (1876) and *Adventures of Huckleberry Finn* (1884).

In 1870, after Nikola had recovered, he moved to the city of Karlovac to live with his aunt and uncle. He attended the Higher Real Gymnasium (high school) there. Unfortunately, Karlovac was a swampy area with lots of mosquitoes. Nikola hadn't been there long before he became sick again. This time he had malaria—an infection caused by mosquito bites.

Nikola's aunt and uncle took care of him, and he got better. He liked his aunt and uncle, but he liked school even more! And as usual, when Nikola liked something, he threw himself into it completely. He worked so hard that it took him only three years to finish the four-year program.

At Higher Real Gymnasium, he was especially impressed with his science classes and science experiments. Every time his professor finished an experiment, Nikola's mind raced with a thousand questions.

Nikola decided he wanted to learn everything he could. He wanted to do his own research. His mind was made up. He was going to become an electrical engineer. An engineer is someone who designs or builds engines. An electrical engineer designs or builds them to work with electricity. He had just one problem, though: His father still wanted him to become a priest. Nikola knew that Milutin wouldn't like it, but he needed to choose his own career path.

Nikola thought it was best to return to Gospić and break the news to Milutin and Djouka. But when Nikola wrote to them, his parents told him not to come. *That's strange,* Nikola thought. He figured they would be happy he had finished his studies a year early. Milutin encouraged him to go on a long hunting trip with some friends. *That's really strange,* Nikola thought. A hunting trip was not something that would interest him, and his parents knew it.

So Nikola traveled the ninety miles to Gospić. What his parents hadn't told him was there was a cholera epidemic in town at the time. Cholera is a serious illness that is caused by bacteria. It is very contagious. And in Nikola's time, it often was deadly.

On his very first day home, Nikola got cholera! He spent the next nine months in bed, and it appeared he would not survive. His parents, who already had lost their son Dane, were stricken with grief. What could they do?

Nikola was near death one day, and his father rushed to his side. "Perhaps I may get well if you will let me study engineering," Nikola said.

His father begged his son to fight for his life. "You will be an engineer," Milutin told him. "Do you hear me? You will go to the best engineering school in the world and you will be a great engineer."

Nikola knew his father meant what he said. And with that to look forward to, he started getting better almost immediately. Less than a week later, he was sitting up in bed. Less than a week after that, he was walking around. He soon recovered, then spent the next year getting stronger.

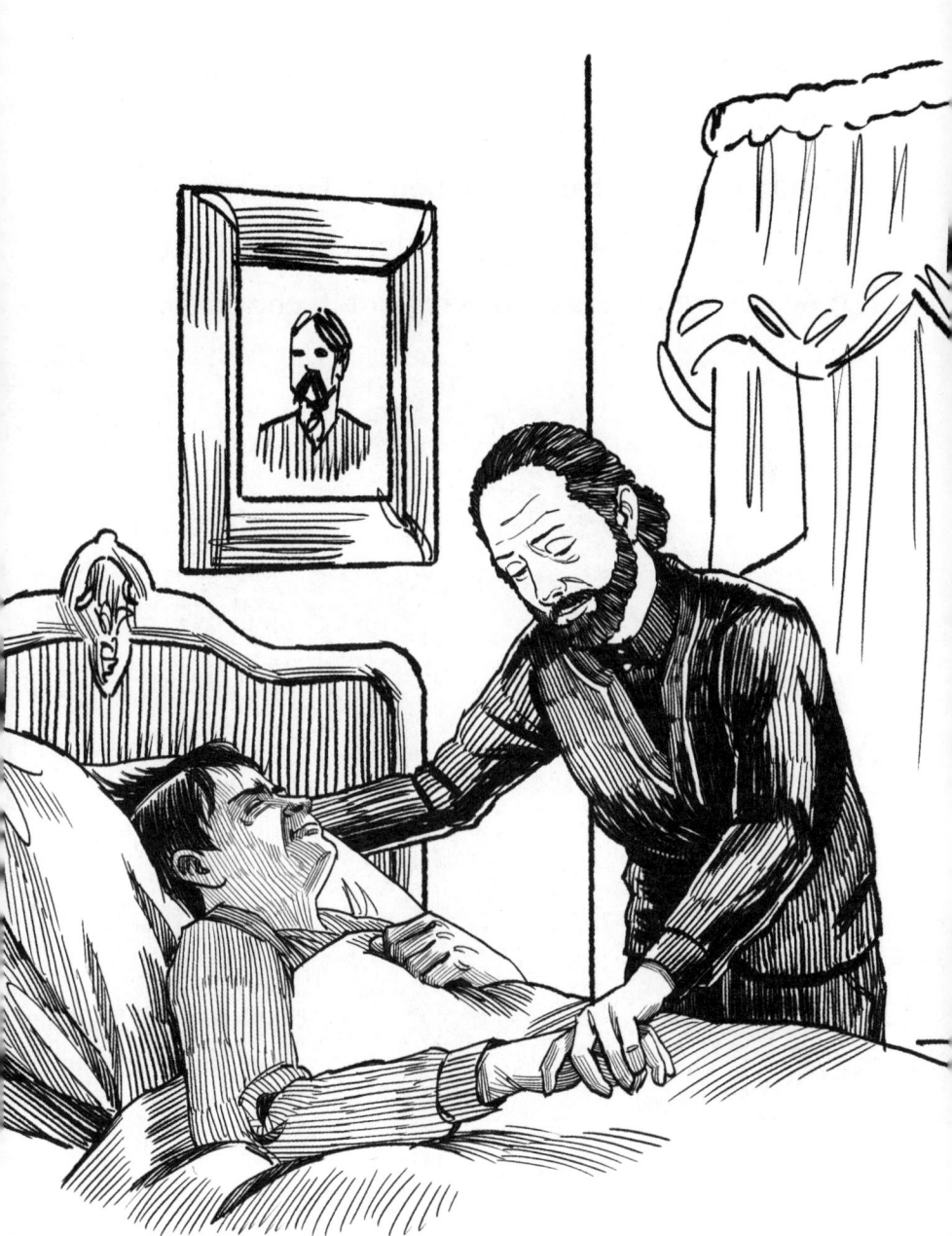

In September 1875, when he was nineteen, Nikola traveled to Graz, Austria, more than two hundred miles from his home. He began his studies in engineering at Polytechnic Institute, now known as Graz University of Technology.

CHAPTER 4
School Days

Nikola—as always—worked tirelessly at Polytechnic Institute. On a typical day, he woke up at three o'clock in the morning. He didn't go to bed until eleven o'clock at night—twenty hours later! Even then, he didn't go right to sleep, but read until he nodded off. Throughout his entire life, Nikola claimed he slept only about two to three hours a night.

Nikola needed all those waking hours. In his first year at the university, he took nine courses, four more than was normal. He studied math, physics, botany, chemistry, and several languages. He never missed a lecture, got the highest grades possible in all of his classes, and even started a school club on Serbian culture. His teachers worried that he was going to overwork himself. One of his professors wrote to Milutin back in Gospić, saying, "Your son is a star of the first rank," but making it clear that Nikola was endangering his health by working too much and sleeping too little.

In his second year at Polytechnic Institute, Nikola concentrated on engineering, limiting his classes to physics, mechanics, and math. On his own time, he studied machines such as dynamos, which produce electricity, and motors, which produce motion or power.

Early in Nikola's second year, a machine arrived at the university from Paris. Nikola's professor demonstrated it to the class. The machine forced an electrical current to move in only one direction, called direct current (DC). Nikola argued that it would be better to let the current flow back and forth because direct current loses more and more power the farther away it gets from its source. A back-and-forth current could keep its same level of power throughout the system. This was called alternating current (AC). It was nothing new, but no one had yet figured out how to make alternating current power a motor.

AC/DC

Current is the flow of an electric charge through a wire. In a direct current (DC), the charge moves in only one direction. In an alternating current (AC), the charge reverses direction, traveling back and forth across the wire.

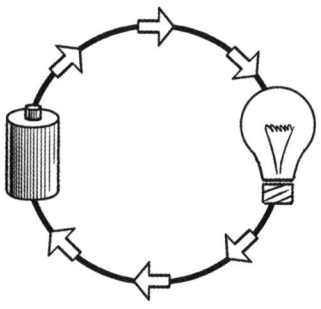

Direct current

This is important because the voltage (the intensity of the electrical current) of alternating current can be controlled and regulated by a transformer. The voltage stays the same in direct current, but only over a short distance.

Alternating current, then, is more useful. A transformer can take a less intense AC current and turn it into a high-voltage current to travel a long distance. At the end of that distance, a transformer can turn the high-voltage current back into a low-voltage current for safe use in homes and businesses.

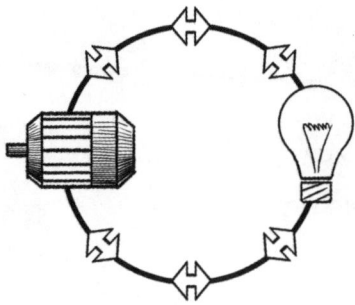

Alternating current

Nikola's professor devoted an entire lecture to why Nikola's theory could not work. "Mr. Tesla will accomplish great things, but he certainly never will do this," he said, speaking about the superiority of DC.

At first, Nikola figured he must be wrong because the professor *had* to know more about machines than he did. But the more he thought about it, the more he believed he was right. "I could not demonstrate my belief at that time," he said, "but it came to me through what I might call instinct." Once again, Nikola was smart enough to see things that others couldn't!

Nikola began building complete machines in his mind. He imagined every nut, bolt, coil, and brush. "The images I saw were perfectly real," he said. He worked on his theory the rest of his second year at the university. But he could not make it work. He became 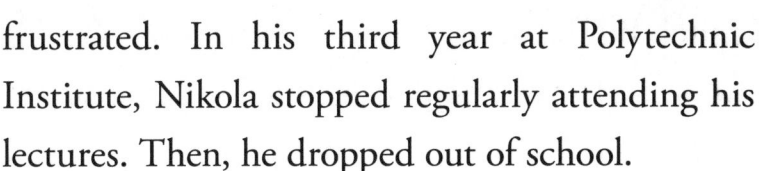 frustrated. In his third year at Polytechnic Institute, Nikola stopped regularly attending his lectures. Then, he dropped out of school.

In 1879, Milutin died at age sixty. Nikola
knew that his father had wanted him to finish
school. But he needed to work to help support his
mother. He decided that he wouldn't go back to
school, and Nikola never earned a college degree.

CHAPTER 5
Coming to America

Nikola immediately began looking for work. His uncle Pajo told him about a friend in Budapest, Hungary. The friend, Uncle Pajo said, was building a telephone exchange. In the early days of the telephone, callers were connected to each other by an operator. The operator pushed electrical cords into slots on a board to make the connection. The machine was called a switchboard. A whole network of switchboards made up a telephone exchange.

Nikola left for Budapest. When he arrived, he found out there was no telephone exchange. His uncle's friend was still trying to build it! There was no job for Nikola. Instead, Nikola went to work for the local telegraph office.

Telegraph machine

Eventually, the telephone exchange was built. Nikola worked as its chief engineer. He made many improvements to the company's equipment, even impressing the inventor of the machinery himself. But Nikola was still more interested in figuring out how to perfect his alternating-current theory.

He imagined a world in which his AC invention powered machines in every factory and in every home. In the early 1880s, very few places had electricity. Not many people understood this mysterious current. It seemed like magic, or like something out of a science-fiction book. Nikola could see a future in which alternating current made electricity an everyday part of life. His AC motor would make that a reality—if he could just make it work!

In February 1882, Nikola was walking in a park in Budapest with a friend. He was reciting poetry when he stopped in his tracks.

"See my engine here!" he exclaimed to his friend. "Watch me reverse it!"

His friend had no idea what Nikola was talking about. He meant that he could now imagine using magnets to reverse the direction of an electric current so that they could produce a turning force in a motor! Nikola excitedly began scratching in the dirt with a stick. He was drawing what had appeared in his mind: the plans for what would become a kind of alternating-current motor called an induction motor.

It *could* be done. Nikola had been right all along. His professor had been wrong.

Nikola was very excited. "For a while I gave myself up entirely to the intense enjoyment of picturing machines," he said. Over the next two months, he imagined all the designs for an alternating-current system—every nut and bolt, for dynamos, motors, transformers, and more.

In April that year, Nikola went to work for the Compagnie Continentale Edison in Paris. It was the French office of the Continental Edison Company, which had been created by the great American inventor Thomas Alva Edison.

One of Nikola's jobs was installing a lighting system at the Paris Opera House. He traveled to work on other lighting systems in Germany and France, too. All of them were DC electrical systems, the only system in use at the time.

In his spare time, Nikola finally built a model of the AC motor he had envisioned months earlier.

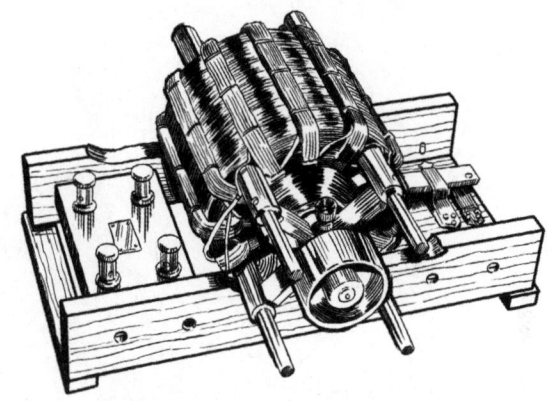

It worked—just as he knew it would. However, he could not find anyone willing to invest the money he needed to build an entire system. No one but Nikola seemed to realize how important it was.

Thomas Alva Edison (1847–1931)

Thomas Edison was an American inventor and businessman. In a long career that began when he started his first business in 1869, he created hundreds of inventions.

Nicknamed "The Wizard of Menlo Park" (Menlo Park was the town in New Jersey where his laboratory was located), his inventions were among the most important in the world. He created the first practical lightbulb and the phonograph, the world's first record player. He also worked to improve other inventions such as the motion-picture camera and the typewriter. Edison's work helped change the way people live.

One of Nikola's bosses in Paris was sent by the company to work for Thomas Edison in New York. He suggested that Nikola do the same. So Nikola made plans to travel by boat to the United States. But shortly before leaving Paris, he was robbed of his money and most of his luggage.

Nikola arrived in New York on June 6, 1884, with four cents in his pocket and a note of introduction from Tivadar Puskás, a Hungarian inventor, to give to Thomas Edison. "I know two great men, and you are one of them," Puskás wrote to Edison. "The other is this young man."

Thomas Edison hired Nikola to work at Edison Machine Works and nicknamed him "the Parisian." He was impressed by Nikola's dedication to his work. In fact, his long hours were much like Edison's. Edison was famous for working around the clock, sometimes stopping only to nap in his clothes for a few hours right in his laboratory.

One day, Edison was leaving the office at five o'clock in the morning after working all night. "Here is our Parisian running around at night," Edison joked. But Nikola wasn't running around. He had spent the entire night fixing the dynamos—the electricity generators—Edison's company had installed on board a ship called the SS *Oregon*. It was one of the first ships with an electric lighting system. Edison was very impressed.

Not long after, Edison gave Nikola the task of redesigning the company's direct-current

A ship worker adjusting the dynamo on the SS *Oregon*

generators—the machines that actually produced all of their electricity. It was a huge job that involved designing more than twenty different machines. If Nikola could do it, he was told, he would be paid a $50,000 bonus!

Nikola worked from ten thirty in the morning until five o'clock the *next* morning every day for nearly a year. When he finally completed the work,

Edison told Nikola that he had been kidding! Talk of the big bonus was all just a joke. "You don't understand our American humor," Edison said. Nikola didn't find it very funny. He had worked day and night to redesign the generators.

Nikola knew it was time to leave Edison Machine Works.

CHAPTER 6
Fame and Fortune

The mid-1880s were an exciting time in New York City. Skyscrapers were being built. The Statue of Liberty arrived as a gift from France in 1885. And parts of Manhattan were being lit by the Edison Electric Illuminating Company of New York.

It was a difficult time for Nikola, however. He was unemployed and broke. He was also alone. His family was halfway around the world. He needed to find a way to put food on the table. Nikola wondered if all his years studying science and mechanics, reading books, and endlessly working through problems in his mind had been a waste of time.

Then Nikola got the chance to earn two dollars per day digging ditches. It turned out to be his big break! The foreman on the job overheard Nikola talking about his AC motor.

He said he knew a man who was an expert electrician. That man's name was Alfred Brown.

When Mr. Brown met Nikola, he was impressed by Nikola's ideas on alternating current. Together with a lawyer named Charles Peck, Brown and Tesla formed the Tesla Electric Company.

They opened a laboratory in New York City in autumn 1886, and worked to develop patents on alternating-current technology. A patent protects the inventor from someone else copying the idea. It creates an authentic record of the date, time, and place of each invention.

That same year, the US government granted Nikola his first patents. In 1888, he presented his system of alternating-current motors and transformers to the American Institute of Electrical Engineers at Columbia University in New York. As usual, he had a clear vision for the future of electricity before anyone else did.

Nikola's patented ideas got the attention of George Westinghouse, the owner of the Westinghouse Electric Company. George was a direct competitor of Thomas Edison's. Nikola explained how his patents could beat Edison in the electricity business.

Edison had brought electricity to parts of Manhattan in 1882, but most Americans

George Westinghouse

were still more than forty years away from
having electricity. They still used gas lamps
and candles to light their homes. Direct current
couldn't travel very far before losing power,
so Edison's DC system required many, many
power plants. Nikola's AC system could supply
electricity to thousands of people with a single
power plant.

George Westinghouse wanted to buy Nikola's alternating-current patents. That gave him the right to use Nikola's ideas as if they were his own.

Westinghouse offered a huge amount for the patents. Some reports say Tesla received about $60,000 for nearly 30 patents. That's about $1.5 million in today's money! Nikola also was to receive payments—called royalties—every time the technology was used in a new system.

Only a few days before his thirty-second birthday in 1888, Nikola accepted Westinghouse's offer. Suddenly, he was a rich man! He sent money home to his mother and his sisters. And he paid the men who had helped him set up the Tesla Company. Nikola had enough left over to do what he really wanted: go back to his lab and work on his ideas.

Nikola had been living in Pittsburgh, Pennsylvania, trying to help the Westinghouse Company make his technology work. But in 1889,

he returned to New York. He opened a new laboratory on Grand Street and moved into the fancy Astor House hotel in New York City.

Nikola invited celebrities and scientists to watch demonstrations of his experiments. He was quite a showman in the lab. He amazed his guests

with demonstrations that looked like magic. In one, he held a glass tube in one hand and a wire coursing with alternating current in the other. The current traveled across his body and into the tube, making it glow with a beautiful light!

Astor House

Astor House was the first luxury hotel in New York. It was built of granite and took up an entire block on Broadway. It had more than three hundred guest rooms on its six floors. And every floor had a bath and toilet—an incredible luxury at the time.

Astor House was built by John Jacob Astor, a wealthy American businessman, in 1836. Eighteen different US presidents stayed there, including Abraham Lincoln, who stopped over for one night on the way to his inauguration in 1861.

Astor House closed in 1913.

Nikola worked on many ideas in his New York lab, including something called the Tesla coil.

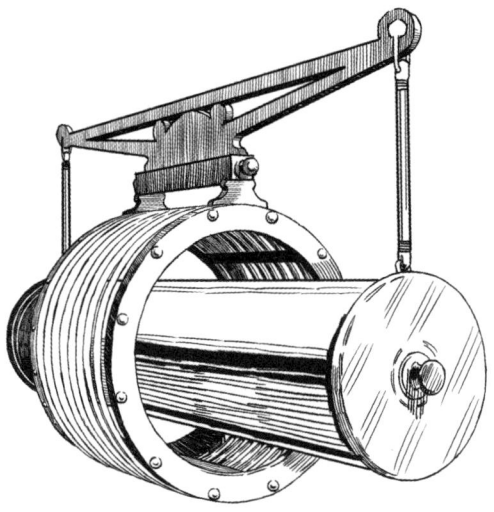

The Tesla coil took a low-voltage alternating current and built it up to a very high-voltage current. Then it released that intense current through a spark that looked like lightning. The spark created an electrical field all around it.

Nikola's amazing imagination was the key to his genius. It made him different from just about every other engineer. Most inventors build a model of a machine and tinker with it until it works.

Nikola, however, first pictured the machine in his mind, down to the very smallest details and exact measurements. He mentally conducted trial operations. He was even able to inspect the machine weeks later, simply by imagining any wear and tear! Only when he absolutely knew it could work did he actually build it.

Much of the time, Nikola worked by himself. But he was not a loner. He not only invited people to his laboratory, he also entertained groups of important scientists at dinner parties. He had many friends who were not scientists, too, including some of the most famous people of his time, such as writers Mark Twain and Rudyard Kipling, and John Jacob Astor IV, the great-grandson of the man who built the Astor House.

The Quirky Inventor

Nikola lived alone for many years. He worked very long hours. And he developed some unique habits.

He only slept two hours each day—but he made sure to find time to do his toe curls in the evenings. He believed that one hundred toe curls for each foot helped the brain.

He avoided coffee, tea, and tobacco.

He ate dinner at exactly the same time every night: 8:10 p.m. After each meal, he wiped every dish and piece of silverware with a clean napkin.

Late in life, he would eat only milk, honey, and bread, and drink only vegetable juice.

Strangely, Nikola could not stand the sight of pearls. He would never touch another person's hair. And he was so afraid of germs that he tried not to shake hands with anyone—ever!

Nikola always dressed well at his dinner parties. He insisted on wearing white gloves and a good suit. He believed a person needed to *look* successful to *be* successful.

Women were very attracted to the blue-eyed genius who stood over six feet tall. Nikola never married, though. He didn't believe an inventor could devote enough attention to his work if he also had a wife. He once told a newspaper reporter that having a wife would take too much time and energy away from an inventor's duty. But then he added, "It's a pity, too, for sometimes we feel so lonely."

CHAPTER 7
War of the Currents

In 1890, the Westinghouse Corporation was in trouble. It was losing money.

To help his friend George Westinghouse, Nikola did something remarkable: He tore up the royalty clause in his contract. That meant he would never earn more money from Westinghouse. Nikola didn't mind. He was more interested in his inventions helping people get electricity than in making more money.

Nikola's partnership with Westinghouse was a big problem for Thomas Edison. At the time, very few homes in the United States had electricity. The average city might have had streetlamps. But people in the countryside wouldn't have even seen them yet. Electrical lines had not yet been set up. There was no way to carry electricity over great distances from the generators. But it was clear that whatever company could find a way to bring electricity to homes in the United States was going to make a lot of money.

Nikola and Westinghouse believed alternating current was the best method. It could travel great distances at high voltage from a large power plant, then be transformed to a lower, safer voltage for homes. Since direct current couldn't be transformed, it could only travel short distances at a safe voltage. Direct current would require a small power plant to be built every mile or so.

Thomas Edison had already started building

those power plants. His first DC power station had opened in New York City in 1882. He knew if AC became standard, he would lose a lot of money on his direct-current stations.

So he tried to convince the public that using alternating current—Tesla's big idea—was a bad and dangerous thing. He worked hard to spread the lie.

Edison distributed thousands of pamphlets that said alternating current was deadly. And horribly, he teamed up with an electrical engineer to electrocute stray dogs with alternating current. And it worked. Investors and public officials became scared of the AC technology. Nikola knew that any electricity—alternating current or direct current—could be dangerous. How could he and Westinghouse prove AC was just as safe as DC?

In 1891, the year Nikola became a citizen of
the United States, he gave another lecture before
the American Institute of Electrical Engineers on
alternating current. The next year, he gave talks
in London and Paris. While in Paris in 1892,
Nikola received a telegram from his uncle Petar
saying that his mother was sick. "I made the
long journey home without an hour of rest,"
Nikola said. His mother died several weeks later
on April 4.

Back in the United States, George Westinghouse scored a huge victory by winning the contract to power the World's Columbian Exposition in Chicago in 1893. Westinghouse got the job because he offered to provide the electricity for less money than Edison did. The first all-electric fair in history was the best chance to show the world that alternating current was safe and effective.

More than two hundred thousand lightbulbs showcased the power of alternating current at the Columbian Exposition. In the Great Hall of Electricity, Nikola wowed onlookers with demonstrations like the ones he had given in his New York City laboratory.

World's Columbian Exposition

The World's Columbian Exposition, sometimes called the Chicago World's Fair, was held from May 1 to October 30, 1893. It celebrated the four hundredth anniversary of Christopher Columbus's arrival in the New World in 1492.

Nearly two hundred temporary buildings were erected over more than six hundred acres to house 65,000 exhibitors from all over the world! Fourteen buildings surrounded a giant pool that represented Columbus's voyage from Spain.

More than 25 million people attended the fair. There were thousands of fun and interesting exhibits. And there were also many new products on display, including Cracker Jack popcorn, Juicy Fruit gum, and Shredded Wheat cereal. And up to 38,000 people a day—more than 1.4 million people in all by the end of the fair—rode the world's first Ferris wheel.

By the end of the six-month exposition, Westinghouse had won over the public. Visitors to the fair could see for themselves how safe and useful the AC lights were. Alternating current soon became the standard technology for delivering electricity to consumers in the United States.

But winning over the public was only a part of the battle in the war of AC versus DC. Actually getting electricity into people's homes would be the more difficult part. Nikola looked to Niagara Falls for answers. Ever since Nikola read about Niagara Falls as a boy, he had been intrigued by hydroelectricity—the force of falling or flowing water to produce power. The rushing force of the fast-moving water turns a wheel called a turbine. The spinning turbine turns a metal shaft in the motor that generates electricity.

Other scientists and engineers long had talked about using the power of Niagara Falls to create electrical energy. However, nothing had ever come of it. The success of AC technology at the World's Columbian Exposition convinced state officials in New York that it just might work. Before the exposition was over, they had awarded Westinghouse Corporation a contract to build turbines and generators for Niagara Falls using Nikola's patents and alternating-current technology!

The first generator was tested in April 1895. The next year, the world's first large-scale hydroelectric power plant officially opened. It immediately began delivering electric power to Buffalo, New York, around twenty miles away. Within just a few years, the range extended all the way to New York City, a distance of over four hundred miles!

CHAPTER 8
Wireless Dreams

Now the East Coast had light! And Nikola had helped open the door to the availability of electrical power for people throughout the United States. By 1925, half of all Americans would be living in the modern age of electricity. Long before then, however, Nikola turned his attention to his next goal: wireless communication.

The telephone had been invented by Alexander Graham Bell in 1876, but it needed wires, of course.

Alexander Graham Bell

And even before Nikola was born, people had been able to communicate long distances by sending signals over a wire. A machine at one end could send an electrical current to a receiver at the other end. The receiver could take the series of short taps (called "dots") and

Samuel F. B. Morse

longer taps ("dashes") and use a code to translate them into words. This machine was the telegraph, and the code was the Morse code. It was named for American Samuel F. B. Morse, an inventor of the telegraph.

But what about the places where there were no wires? What if a ship in the middle of the ocean needed help and wanted to signal ashore? Nikola knew that the air is filled with invisible electromagnetic waves called radio waves. Instead of using wires to carry those signals of dots and dashes, Nikola pictured using radio waves to carry them.

In 1895, just as thirty-nine-year-old Nikola was preparing to transmit a signal by radio waves for a distance of fifty miles, Guglielmo Marconi sent and received his first signals without wires and was awarded a patent for radio technology!

Guglielmo Marconi

Nikola had been so close to perfecting his transmissions. But a fire had ruined his New York laboratory.

Nikola had been giving lectures about using radio waves to send messages and sound since the early 1890s. He demonstrated a remote-controlled boat using radio waves in New York in 1898. The people who watched it were amazed! Nikola had to take the boat apart to show there were no tricks hidden inside.

Nikola talked about a wireless world in which "we shall be able to communicate with each other instantly, irrespective of distance." And the device? "A man will be able to carry one in his vest pocket." How right Nikola was! That sounds like a modern cell phone!

Nikola had missed his chance to be the first to send a wireless signal a long distance. But why stop at sending a small amount of information such as the message Marconi sent? Why not use those waves to send large amounts of information? Information such as pictures, music, and voices. That sounds a lot like the Internet!

As usual, Nikola's ideas were way ahead of his time. But technology had to catch up to those ideas first. To help create the technology, he conducted bigger and bigger experiments. And Nikola's high-voltage, high-frequency experiments were becoming too large and too dangerous for his New York City lab.

In 1899, Nikola moved to Colorado Springs, Colorado, where he built a large laboratory. It included a gigantic Tesla coil fifty-two feet in diameter! It created an enormous electrical field that allowed Nikola to light lamps many miles away without wires.

In 1900, Nikola returned to New York. He built a 187-foot-high tower at his lab on Long Island, in an area called Wardenclyffe. He hoped the tower would be the first to send signals—and power—wirelessly to anywhere in the world.

Wardenclyffe Tower

Nikola's plan for Wardenclyffe didn't work. In 1905, he was forced to close down his laboratory.

Nikola was still only forty-nine years old. But after Wardenclyffe closed, he seemed to disappear from the scientific community. In May 1917, though, he was presented the Edison Medal, the highest honor presented by the American Institute

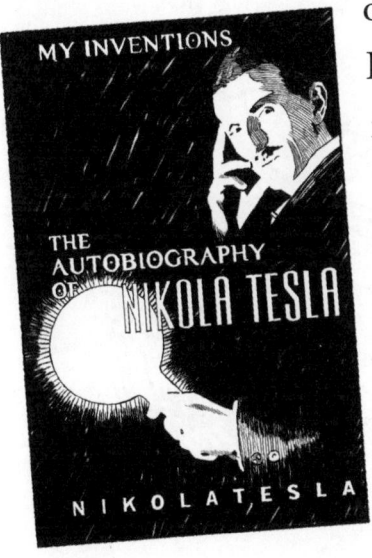

of Electrical Engineers. In 1919, Nikola wrote the first of a series of articles for *Electrical Experimenter* magazine. An editor later combined the articles into a Tesla autobiography called *My Inventions*.

Nikola continued to work on projects that interested him. In 1920, he designed a type of aircraft that could take off vertically like a helicopter but would fly like an airplane.

Who Invented Radio?

Guglielmo Marconi

At 12:30 p.m. on December 12, 1901, Italian inventor and electrical engineer Guglielmo Marconi listened intently on his earphone at a desk in

Newfoundland, Canada. He heard a series of three dots. That is the Morse code for the letter *s*. The message had been sent from a transmitting station Marconi built in Cornwall, England, more than two thousand miles away. It was the first radio transmission to cross the Atlantic Ocean.

Marconi formed a wireless telegraph company and began improving his ability to send messages via radio signal. But his transmitters needed a Tesla coil to work.

Nikola sued Marconi a couple of years later for using his technology. The US Patent Office ruled in Nikola's favor in 1903. But it reversed its decision in 1904. Marconi is credited as the inventor of radio transmission, although in fact it was a combined effort of many people, especially Nikola Tesla.

It was only a design, but, like everything else, Nikola was certain it would work because he already had "tested" it in his mind. Once again, Nikola was ahead of his time. Years later, a very similar aircraft was built by the US military.

As he got older, Nikola lived a more solitary life. He spent his days taking long walks in New York and feeding the pigeons in Bryant Park.

He moved from hotel to hotel—sometimes because the maids complained about the pigeons he brought back to the room, and sometimes because he was unable to pay the bills.

Finally, the Westinghouse Corporation, perhaps out of gratitude for when Nikola tore up his royalty contract many years before, agreed to pay for his room at the Hotel New Yorker.

On his birthday each year, Nikola invited reporters to the hotel to talk about his new ideas and plans. But his ideas were getting stranger and stranger. One year, he talked about a "death ray" machine that he believed would end all wars. Another year, he spoke about his contact with other planets. He also hinted at a major new power source he *might* be developing.

Because his decision to tear up his royalty contract with Westinghouse cost him millions of dollars, Nikola was broke. When he died at age eighty-six in 1943, he was also alone. His decision not to get married meant that he had no family at his side.

Even though this sounds like a very sad ending, Nikola's reputation grew after his death, and people began to honor him for his brilliance and his many scientific developments.

In 1943, a US Supreme Court decision confirmed that Nikola had contributed to the invention of radio. In 1960, a unit of measurement (to describe the strength of a magnetic field) was named the tesla. And in 1975, Nikola was inducted into the National Inventors Hall of Fame. He was honored on a US postage stamp in 1983.

His face appeared on both the five-dinar bill and the five-million-dinar bill in Yugoslavia, as well as the Serbian hundred-dinar bill.

Tesla coils are on display in places such as the Griffith Observatory in Los Angeles and the Museum of Science and Industry in Chicago. Tesla, Inc. is a line of luxury electric cars named in his honor. Many modern technological advances, like cell phones, Internet, GPS, radio, television, radar, and neon signs, are built on Nikola's groundbreaking work and ideas.

Part creative genius, part mad scientist, and completely ahead of his time, Nikola Tesla made the electric age possible.

Timeline of Nikola Tesla's Life

1856 — Nikola Tesla is born on July 10 in Smiljan, in what is modern-day Croatia

1870 — Moves to Karlovac and begins studying at Higher Real Gymnasium

1882 — Invents alternating-current motor

1884 — Moves to New York and begins working for Thomas Edison

1885 — Applies for his first US patent, on an improved arc lamp

1888 — Sells alternating-current patents to George Westinghouse

1891 — Becomes a US citizen

1893 — Working with the Westinghouse Electric Corporation, provides electricity for the Columbian Exposition (the World's Fair) in Chicago

1895 — The power station he designed at Niagara Falls begins operating

1896 — Patents inventions relating to radio

1898 — Demonstrates remote-controlled boat in New York City

1907 — Elected to the New York Academy of Sciences

1917 — Receives 1916 Edison Medal from the American Institute of Electrical Engineers

1919 — Begins writing his autobiography, *My Inventions*, in *Electrical Experimenter* magazine

1943 — Dies of a heart attack in New York City on January 7

Timeline of the World

1860 — Abraham Lincoln is elected the sixteenth president of the United States

1861 — The American Civil War begins, and lasts until 1865

1876 — Alexander Graham Bell invents the telephone

1877 — Thomas Edison invents the phonograph

1880 — Wabash, Indiana, becomes the first American city to use electric streetlights

1886 — The Statue of Liberty is dedicated in New York

1892 — Ellis Island opens in New York Harbor

1903 — The Wright brothers fly a plane at Kitty Hawk, North Carolina

1912 — The ocean liner *Titanic* sinks on its first voyage

1914 — World War I begins in Europe, and lasts until 1918

1919 — A major flu epidemic, which began in 1918, kills as many as fifty million people worldwide

1929 — The New York stock market crashes, and the Great Depression begins

1932 — Franklin Delano Roosevelt is elected president of the United States for the first of a record four terms

1941 — The United States enters World War II after Pearl Harbor in Hawaii is attacked

Bibliography

*Books for young readers

Carlson, W. Bernard. *Tesla: Inventor of the Electrical Age.* Princeton, NJ: Princeton University Press, 2013.

Cawthorne, Nigel. *Tesla: The Life and Times of an Electric Messiah.* New York: Chartwell Books, 2014.

*Dommermuth-Costa, Carol. *Nikola Tesla: A Spark of Genius.* Minneapolis: Lerner Publications Company, 1994.

*Hardyman, Robyn. *Nikola Tesla and Thomas Edison* (**Dynamic Duos of Science**). New York: Gareth Stevens Publishing, 2015.

Kent, David J. *Tesla: The Wizard of Electricity.* New York: Sterling, 2013.

*Rusch, Elizabeth. *Electrical Wizard: How Nikola Tesla Lit Up the World.* Somerville, MA: Candlewick Press, 2013.

Tesla, Nikola. *My Inventions and Other Writings.* New York: Penguin Books, 2011.

*Yount, Lisa. *Nikola Tesla: Harnessing Electricity.* New York: Chelsea House, 2012.